First Light

First Light

Seeking Cosmic Life

Don C. Nix, J.D., Ph.D.

iUniverse, Inc.
Bloomington

iUniverse books may be ordered through booksellers or by contacting:

iUniverse
1663 Liberty Drive
Bloomington, IN 47403
www.iuniverse.com
1-800-Authors (1-800-288-4677)

ISBN: 978-1-4502-9152-1 (sc)
ISBN: 978-1-4502-9153-8 (ebook)

Printed in the United States of America

iUniverse rev. date: 02/09/2011

Dedication

To Benjamin Honey, my Welsh grandson, a bundle of fierce energy who just turned five. I think that we will have little opportunity to get to know each other, but you have my blessings and my love as you go forward through the arc of your life into a future that I cannot imagine, even in my dreams. I won't be there to see you in that future life, but I can imagine you there now as a powerful, compassionate and highly developed man. You are the heir of two Texas families, cattle-ranchers and frontier preachers, whose ancestors came across the U.S. after the Civil War, and carved out new lives in a land that was still frontier-rough. You are from good stock, as we say in Texas about our cattle and ourselves.

Your grandfather,
Far
Sonoma, California
January, 2011

Contents

Introduction

We are evolving rapidly. However, it is anyone's guess whether we can grow up fast enough to avoid destroying ourselves. Everywhere we look there is massive change, but the amount of change required to save ourselves is monumental. We must literally change the worldview of billions of people. We must have a leap in evolution that takes us to another way of viewing reality. And we must do it quickly.

Jean Gebser, the great historian of the evolution of human consciousness, identified four distinct phases in human development. He believed that we are at the end of the fourth phase, which he called the mental, which began about 500 B.C. He said that at the end of a phase two things happen. The next leap in evolution begins to appear, bringing new capacities that have never existed before, which truly change the human prospect. Second, the dying phase becomes toxic and dysfunctional, worn out and distorted by its over-emphasis of its central feature. This pretty much describes where we are today, trapped in our heads, over-intellectual and out of touch with our hearts and our bodies, and trapped in separateness. Our personal lives are full of despair, desolation and alienation, and our institutions are functioning poorly.

Quantum physics has thrown open a doorway that might give us a way out. In characterizing the universe as a singularity without parts, a "Unified Field," it has perhaps laid the foundation for a new worldview that is beyond separateness. If we can grow ourselves into a new awareness that we are an integral part of the Field of Being, and that the entire Field is alive, conscious, intelligent, creative and unfolding, then perhaps our separateness can yield to being subsumed in Something sacred and miraculous. Life and reality would look quite different through this lens. It is appearing now. It is coming. The question is whether we have enough time.

1

First light
cuts through the darkness,
and silhouettes the eastern hill.
Another day is coming
to this chaotic Earth.
Radiance arrives and
begins to spill
over pain and grief and sorrow.
Eternity is bringing Its glowing light
and perhaps a better tomorrow.

2

Rainbows all around me
as I spill myself into my life,
but my eyes are too dim,
and my heart is too weak,
and my soul is too distant
to see them.
I must
grow myself larger and deeper.
I must
open myself to the Unseen.
I must
touch the beauty beneath the crust.
I must
see the rainbows that live in the Source,
thrown up by the shimmering Force.

3

You are chimera.
I am too.
The world around us is virtual,
at least from a certain
point of view.
We are all particles dancing,
now here,
now there,
now nowhere.
They have thrown up the world in their play,
and brought our bodies from the void
to dance our life away.
How strange to be caught
in this rhythm,
compelled to dance and dance.
How strange to be roughed up
and tumbled around
in a chimerical world
of drama and chance.

4

What impact can one voice have
in a world gone deaf, dumb and blind?
What's the point of singing your aria
if the audience is lost in mania?
Perhaps the reply is a simple thing.
If you can be focused and strong,
just stand on the stage,
your own center stage,
amid the surrounding cacophony,
and open your mouth and sing your song,
and sing,
and sing,
and sing.

5

The geyser is erupting.
Pushed by forces
in the deep, dark earth
the boiling liquid bursts forth.
What is there to understand?
What is there to do in this dream?
Just stand in awe
of the Power unseen
that fuels the erupting stream.

6

I am a leaf
floating down the stream,
carried by moving water.
I drift along
in my usual way,
absorbed in the passing scene.
Sometimes I must pass through rapids,
and then I will have a quieter view.
I drift along
in my usual way,
aware that I'm headed
toward the Bay,
and the Bay empties into the Ocean.
My final destination is waiting for me,
the wondrous Open Sea.

7

I notice that you are beating me up,
and burning me and pounding me.
Is it proper for me to ask why?
Am I supposed to be learning something here?
Am I in a school for wayward souls?
Am I expected to move up a grade,
and move deeper,
and touch Your Source?
I'm willing.
I'm eager to graduate.
I'm giving it my all right now.
But is it OK to pummel me so
for not knowing why or how?

8

Are you trapped in your head today?
Have you put all your chips on the intellect?
Do you notice your life is dry?
Are you confronting daily emptiness?
Do you ever ask yourself why?
The mind is a wonderful tool,
but it's not enough to live this life.
There is more here than the mind can see.
There are levels of life that cannot be
experienced with the head.
Expand yourself now to include the heart.
Wake up your cells and your body too.
This won't take you clear to Being,
but at least it's a very good start.

9

It's five a.m.
Do you know where your soul is?
When did you last see it?
When did you last feel
that you needed it?
Have you lost your bridge
to ecstasy,
and not even noticed
that it was gone?

10

As I open myself,
I am flooded
with the vastness of being alive,
with the electricity
of the Livingness,
that fires my nervous system.
What gift can compare to this?
What grace is pouring on me?
What thing in this world
that I can see
can match this boiling ecstasy?

11

I open myself to the Invisible One,
intimate,
warm,
potent,
dynamic,
enlivening.
I see through the surface of things.
I pass through the crust of the world,
and my heart fills,
and over-spills,
with the substance
of throbbing and pulsing Life.

12

We only see the obvious,
and we think that's all there is.
But beneath the
beautiful world of Earth,
a Radiant Realm abides,
filled with livingness,
and awareness,
and power,
and infinite creativity.
Wake up your sleeping heart.
Make your perceptions razor keen.
Give yourself a brand-new start,
and open your eyes to the vast Unseen.

13

We are creatures of both light and dark.
We go from one to the other,
now shrouded in velvet night,
now lit by the radiant Sun.
We'd rather have day
because that is the way
we think we can see more clearly.
But reality is not just the one,
the radiance of the exploding Sun.
The night has its gifts to give us too.
Mystery pulsing around us.

14

Dancing in the dark,
we push our way
into a new day,
filled with trepidation.
We'd like to nail the future down.
We'd like to have it guaranteed,
but this is the wrong Cosmos for that.
Our lives are full of uncertainty,
and fear and vulnerability.
Safety is just an illusion.
We must keep pushing forward.
We must greet our life head-on.
We must meet the unfolding universe
just as it actually is.

15

I am not just a head on a stick.
I have a robust body too,
and a full, rich heart full of feeling
and a belly full of will.
I want to use all of my treasures.
I want to make myself whole.
In the time that I'm here
I will move past my fear
and embrace this opera
that is called my life.

16

Something is holding the world in place
and knitting it all together.
Something is spinning the Earth in space
and dancing it around the sun.
Something is beating my heart.
Something is breathing my breath.
I bow to that subtle Something
that I know I can never see.
I open my heart to Its grace
in letting me be the little me.

17

Fortuitously I'm here.
Fortuitously I see.
Fortuitously I breathe the air
that's placed here just for me.
I see that the world is constructed
to fit perfectly all together.
I see the design of a Master,
an Architect of renown,
with an eye for beauty and meaning
and resources that astound.

18

I breathe the air without thinking.
My hearts beats too without thinking.
I think my thoughts
as I move through my day
in my unconscious and habitual way,
unaware of limitless miracles
that envelop and enfold my stay.

19

What will we do when the air around
has become too toxic to breathe?
Where will we go when our sun-filled cities
have become too trash-filled to live in?
What will we eat when our every food
is too poisoned to sustain our life?
When will we wake up and truly see
the future that's coming to be?

20

There are diamonds in my head,
sparkling,
glinting,
shimmering,
and sending out rays of light
to every point
and in every direction.
This consciousness is not just mine.
It's a gift from the Great Divine.
I should fall on my knees to receive it.
Grace is raining upon me now.

21

How can I give my gift?
I guess I must find it first.
But that aside, how could I know
that the world wants what I have to offer?
It seems to have gone so astray.
It seems to be so off the tracks.
But there must be some creative way
that I can have my say,
and have it heard
and registered,
in this whirling, deafening cacophony.

22

Life swirls itself all around me
through form,
through space,
through thought.
We're in an Ocean of Livingness,
sentient,
intelligent,
dynamic,
more wondrous than the lustrous dreams
of sacredness that I sought.

23

I think I have a vocation.
In these latter years
before I go
I see that I have something to do.
It has been delivered to me
outside my will,
and outside my sight.
It appeared as if overnight.
It seized me.
It shook me.
It whirled me around,
and, to my amazement,
I suddenly found
I had a profounder
and deeper insight.
Who is the doer here?

24

I feel life's sweetness in my heart.
It is there, expanding, in my heart.
I open to its subtle joy,
and tingle with its richness.
It's been there all along, it seems,
but I have been preoccupied
with serious things,
like the cost of beef,
and a new pair of shoes,
and the list of chores
that I plan to do.
I haven't had time just to be,
to revel in feeling the pulse of life,
but now I can truly see,
in this present moment at least,
what's truly important,
what's truly here,
and how I might finally get free.

25

The Earth is waiting for us to grow up,
patiently,
peacefully,
serenely waiting.
It has followed our arc
from the trees to right now.
It has filled our stomachs
and fired our minds.
It has nurtured us faithfully.
It has held us tenderly.
Now it's waiting for us
to stop our fit,
and contain our rage,
to settle ourselves in maturity,
to realize in our minds and depths
that it is the source of our ecstasy.
When will we truly wake up?

26

We're engaged in metamorphosis.
We have learned to call it aging.
As the days go by
and the seasons pass
our bodies slowly change,
until at last
we are faded and old.
We've become a vintage brew.
We watch this happen slowly,
wondrous and in amazement.
We never thought it would happen to us,
but the cycle of life is inexorable.
It applies to us as well.
We are given this gift,
the gift of our life,
and then we are challenged
to give it up.

27

There is livingness in the dark.
Though we feel it's right
to prefer the light
the dark has its gifts to offer.
There's mystery there,
and potential,
and though there's nothing to see,
the dark is harboring the future.
It will burst into being
in our lovely world,
and demand its right to be.

28

Shower me with your blessings.
Fire my little brain.
Give me Your guidance
so I can find
the truth of my self,
the truth of the world,
and the truth of Your Cosmic Mind.

29

Make me a beautiful thing.
Craft me with all your skill.
Expand my capacities.
Fire my mind and body too.
Amp up my flagging will.
Don't do this just for me.
There must be a larger span.
Open my eyes so I can see
and serve Your unfolding plan.

30

I'm beginning to dimly see
that I'm becoming what I must be.
The Cosmos is unfolding Itself,
unfolding our world,
and slowly unfolding the miniscule me.

31

I raise my eyes to the stars,
whirling through blackest night.
I sense into the Majesty
that hovers just beyond my sight.
There's richness here for me.
There's depth and pure delight.
There's joy in being able to see
into the heart of Sublimity.

32

I am a tiny particle
in the Field of Cosmic Light.
I am swirled by the winds
that blow through space
in the blackness of the night.
I see that I'm searching incessantly
for my place in this shimmering, sacred Sea.
I'm trying to touch the Invisible One,
the Living Infinity.

33

My themes are few.
My needs are huge.
I write my words.
I follow my urge.
I'm unfolding something new.
Something is coming clear.
The Invisible looms into sight.
My soul stirs itself
and then takes flight,
and I follow,
follow,
follow.

34

Take me.
Use me.
Fill my heart.
Give me great hands of power.
Throw me into
the river of life.
Enlist me now
in this darkest hour.

35

My heart opens.
Tears spill.
And I know in this moment
that I'm truly alive.
An opening heart
is a brand-new start
in the unfolding of my soul.

36

Beneath the forms that I see,
beneath the world around me,
a realm of Living Light resides,
brilliant,
shimmering,
tracing the world in Its every curve.
This is Life in its purest form.
This is what lies deep and unseen.
I can see It in my mind's eye.
I can see Its brilliant forms.
I'd like to touch It with my hands,
but I know that
It's far beyond my reach.

37

I cannot seem to sustain
a lofty, expansive view.
I can get there for a moment.
I can even see something new.
But then in the very next moment
I fall back into the smallness
of my tiny, self-absorbed mind.
The veils close tightly around me,
and I lose my fragile view
of the miracle of existence
and the glowing Cosmic Sea.

38

I am bigger than I dreamed.
While I fretted and feared
that my life would end,
Something was coming to extend
my universe and my depth.
It burst me through my limits.
It spun me all around.
It delivered visions to my sight.
It came with Its boiling dynamic might,
and made,
for just one moment,
my life deep, rich, and profound.

39

The Earth and I
are spinning through space,
but I don't know
where we're going.
There must be
some meaning here.
There must be
some reason for my fear.
I am carried along
on this journey through night,
whether I truly desire
to travel or not.
Some Force is unfolding me
and my life,
but It's totally out of my sight.

40

Mysterious Force,
can you tell me, please,
what is Your interest in me?
Why have You brought me
to this Earth,
and what am I supposed to do?
I am willing to co-operate,
to play my role,
to sing my song,
but I don't have any instructions,
and You seem to be so silent.
Give me a signal of some kind.
Don't leave me in this bind.

41

Storm clouds are gathering now.
While we dreamed our dreams
of separateness,
we drifted into trouble.
Our minds were too closed
and our hearts were too small,
and we were too self-obsessed.
We couldn't see miracles around us
or see Reality at all.
Our limited primate perspective
grew to be immensely destructive.
Now we wait
and we watch
and we shiver,
as the future turns dark,
as the portents come clear,
as the pay-off time draws near.

42

Dawn breaks
as I sit in my chair,
as I wait through the years
for my life to begin.
How will I know
when it's started?
What will I do with it then?
Why am I caught
in this endless wait,
and how can I wake
to the sparkling Now?
Life is what happens
between cups of tea.

43

In this moment of silence
my heart opens to Life,
not the little life
of my self-absorbed mind,
with its supermarket,
and shoe-store,
and television,
and free-way.
I mean the Real Life,
the Life of swirling galaxies
and exploding stars
and welling, unfolding destiny.
I am a traveler here,
constantly journeying
from the mundane and insignificant
to regions of vast Sublimity.
Come travel with me.

44

If I can relax my mind
and stop thinking incessantly
about myself,
perhaps Something alive
can enter,
Something mysterious and grand,
Something conscious and enlivening,
Something that can blast me,
in a moment,
from this tiny self
into the galaxies.

45

We are the first humans
to see across light-years,
to observe the volcanic
and explosive processes
of creation of the Cosmos,
and to burst through
the boundaries of our mind
into the limitless space of Life.
Wake up.
Wake up.
Wake up to the miracles of now.

46

The dark is rising.
We can see it.
We can feel it.
We're afraid of it.
We recoil from it.
We search for a way forward
that is lit by points of light,
a way through this tunnel of darkness
made by our blooming mistakes.
Though we have no map to follow,
Eternity is not perturbed.
There is no darkness here
that the light cannot swallow.

47

I want to do something significant.
It need not be astounding.
I want to know
that I passed this way,
and gave my gifts
to a future day.
I want to have meant something.

48

We hunger for meaning and depth
as we hunger for water and food.
As we make our way
through a clouded day
and unfold our little life,
we want to be significant,
we want to somehow matter.
We want to have something
to show for our pain,
some kind of result
for playing the game,
but where can we find it
and what is its name?
Raise your eyes to the Cosmic Sea.
It holds all the meaning
that you can be.
It's the source of all your value.

49

I am in here
and the world is out there.
We are only one
though we appear to be two.
I cannot trust my eyes.
My senses will deceive.
There is a deeper reality
than the world that I perceive.
I must reach with my heart,
it seems,
to get the truthful view.

50

Life blooms its way into being.
A flower is bursting here.
All around me
the petals unfurl.
All around me
aromas swirl.
How strange to be inside a flower
that is changing as I gaze,
that is throwing me up
and firing my mind
as I travel through my days.

51

The Earth is our mother,
our mater,
our matter.
The Earth is the source of our life.
We come from its body,
its carbon,
its minerals,
from the depths of its being
we breathe.
We're given our water,
our food and our air.
When will we wake to its care?

52

Some time ago
we were blown to Earth
as carbon molecules,
sent into space
by exploding stars
to find our rightful place.
Now we're here,
we're alive,
we're fully formed,
and our mind is awake and aware.
What should we do?
We're ready to go,
to play our part
in the Cosmic show.

53

Between the darkness and the light
the world turns Prussian Blue.
In a time of silence and waiting
it makes itself anew.
Potential then builds
for life to resume.
The unfolding will now recommence.
The world wakes up to its future.
Another miraculous day on Earth.

54

I want to be bigger than this.
I want to see deeper than this.
I yearn to be enveloped
and absorbed into Vast Being.
How can I burst my bounds?
How can I reach to the skies?
How can I finally see
the Miracle that is throwing up me?

55

I sit alone in the dawn.
The fire is licking the logs.
I try to see
through the crust of the world,
but it seems to be
beyond me.
Yesterday I could do it.
Then, I touched Majesty.
But today I'm different in some way.
I seem to change every day.

56

I have my preferences for my life.
I have an agenda too.
I know now
just how
I want everything to go.
I know what I want to do,
but Something else is active here.
I'm not the driver of this car.
I watch from the back seat,
a little breathless,
not knowing what
will come into view.

57

Give me a moment of ecstasy.
Fill my heart with bliss.
I'm empty and dry
and that is why
I'm asking for your touch.
I know you are here in the room
and in the Cosmos out there.
I know you're aware
of my yearning heart.
I know you can give me
a brand-new start,
and lift my spirits,
and clear my eyes,
and make my little life bloom.

58

Is it too much to ask
to know why I'm here?
I don't want to bother
but I want to push farther
in pressing my basic question.
Can You give just a hint
of what You've in mind?
The people around me
are just as confused.
We're trying to do our best,
but we need a little guidance here.
We need to know why
and perhaps what and how.
Can You give us a little something now?

59

The world is spinning out of control.
We've pushed it to the limit.
We thought we were in the driver's seat.
We thought that we could handle it.
But now we see
that there must be
a massive re-organization.
We need to change our ways,
and fast,
to avoid the coming devastation.

60

Dawn is coming again.
Apollo's chariot rides through the sky.
The world is waiting
for the warmth and light
and sustenance and life
that issues from on high.

61

I search myself for the next poem.
I seem to be empty and dry.
Perhaps I look in the wrong place.
Perhaps that's the reason why.
I'm not the source of this welling.
I'm only a conduit.
It comes from the Earth
and the space and the sky.
My job is to listen to it.

62

Life pulses and blooms
in its own quiet way
before my astonished eyes.
Light comes in the morning
and rages all day
and then in the evening dies.
We live our lives.
The cycles march on.
We're learning to see the Sacred.
We're coming awake
so that we can take
our place in unfolding Miracle.

63

Rain on the roof.
The Earth drinks it in,
thirstily,
greedily,
needily.
This water is needed for life.
The Earth is providing what's needed.
It all fits together
in a master plan.
The processes work
so that all life can
continue to flourish and bloom
on the Earth.

64

What I thought was solid
is space.
What I thought was inert
lives.
What I thought was empty
is full.
What is invisible around me
gives
my life and the world its meaning.
My eyes are only just opening now.
I yearn to touch Livingness now,
if I only knew just how.

65

There must be a Master Plan here.
In moments I see that my fear
is grounded in separateness.
If I am part of a vast, living Sea
then nothing can harm the little me.
I am rooted in Eternity.
I can only lose my form.

66

Each moment is filled
with sacredness,
as the Cosmos unfolds Itself.
What never was appears,
perfectly designed,
perfectly collated
with the vastness that already is.
The tapestry is coherent.
The miracle comes into view.
There's something astounding
at work here.
Something deep and rich and true.

67

I'm held, for this moment,
in invisible arms.
I have been for quite a long time.
For decades the balances
have been kept
that keep me on this Earth.
I am a creature of miracle.
I breathe.
I think.
I digest my food.
I'm part of a living Cosmic Sea
that surrounds and nourishes me.

68

The blackest night
must yield to day,
because that is the way
the Earth is turning
round the sun.
The Cosmos is dancing
Its dance of One.
The flower of Life
is blooming Itself
into ever-new configurations.

69

I relax myself.
I open myself.
I empty my mind
so that I can find
the jewel beneath the crust.
There is so much here
that I cannot see,
but can only feel,
and I want to be
enveloped in Its magnificence.

70

How can I get finally free
of this self-absorbed ego
that purports to be me?
I've done battle with it for years.
I have watched its operations.
I have endured its machinations.
Now I'm clear that
I want to move beyond.
I want to move into something deeper.
I'm giving it my very best shot now.
I want to blow through my edges.

71

In grace I was born.
I grew.
I developed.
In grace I endured
the fires of the world.
In grace I became
the one I am now.
In looking back
I cannot tell how
it happened, or why
or what I learned.

72

We are in the grip
of Something here
that is deep and profound
and powerful.
It's in the air all around us.
It pulsates in our blood.
It beats our heart.
It fires our mind
and potentially enables us to find
a way to perceive Its invisible Life.

73

Now that I've had my day,
I have just a few things to say.
We have all been asleep
for far too long.
We must open our eyes
and sing our song.
We're surrounded by miracle here.
We must see It
and feel It
and give It Its place.
It will change our little lives.
When we expand ourselves
and It becomes dear,
It will give us a pathway
out of our fear.

74

What if I could deepen?
What if I could take
this self-absorbed mind
and blast it into the stars?
If I blew through my edges,
perhaps I could see
the greater being
that I could be
before I step off
to Eternity.

75

The body is a tuning fork,
vibrating with the melodies
of Universal Life.
We overlook its resonance.
Trapped in our heads
and ringing the changes
on our eternal problems,
we are blind and entirely miss
this fount of ecstasy limitless.

76

How can I deepen
and expand myself?
What must I do
to break free?
How can I reach this Power
that is surrounding and holding me?
I know I must get
beyond my mind.
I must grow out of separateness.
I know that I must somehow find
a way to touch this infinite bliss.

77

I thought my heart
would burst in wonder.
I thought I might explode.
In getting free
of the ego me,
for just a moment
I thought I rode
the blazing Sun cross a starry sky
and through a thundering heaven.
Then the vision dimmed
and I found myself,
as often I have before,
in my chair,
in the dawn,
with fire burning there
in the fireplace,
and in my grateful heart.